629.13　ENFIELD LIBRARIES　04/24

I Bet I Can ...
FLY A PLANE

Tom Jackson and Pipi Sposito

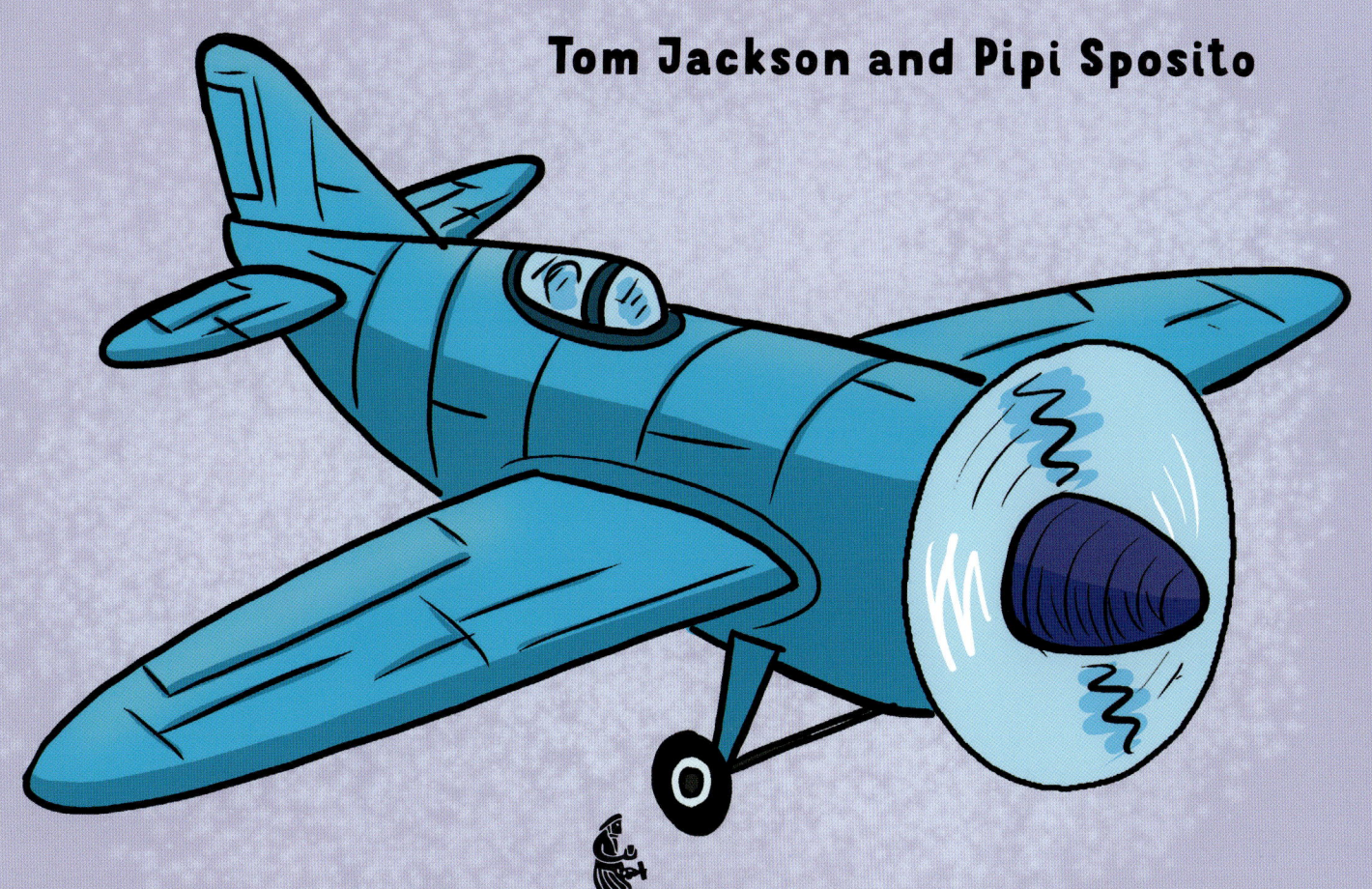

WAYLAND

First published in Great Britain in 2024
by Wayland
© Hodder and Stoughton, 2024
All rights reserved

Credits:
Series Editor: Melanie Palmer
Design: Lisa Peacock
Illustrations: Pipi Sposito

ISBN hb 978 1 5263 2544 0
ISBN pb 978 1 5263 2545 7
Printed and bound in China

Wayland
An imprint of
Hachette Children's Group
Part of Hodder and Stoughton
Carmelite House
50 Victoria Embankment
London EC4Y 0DZ

An Hachette UK Company
www.hachette.co.uk
www.hachettechildrens.co.uk

London Borough of Enfield

91200000810595

Askews & Holts   11-Apr-2024

J629.13 JUNIOR NON-F

ENORDN

Contents

Look, up in the sky!	4–5
Making the wings	6–7
What went wrong? & How does it work?	8-9
What shall I make it with?	10-11
What went wrong? & How does it work?	12-13
The need for speed	14-15
What went wrong? & How does it work?	16-17
What goes up ... must come down	18-19
What went wrong? & How does it work?	20-21
Help! I need to stay in control	22-23
What went wrong? & How does it work?	24-25
Wow, I can fly!	26-27
More flying machines	28-29
How to become a pilot	30
Quiz	31
Glossary /Index	32

Look, up in the sky!

The first plane was invented over 120 year ago and people have been flying in them ever since. Planes give us an amazing view from high above the ground, They can swoop and loop through the air, and we use them to travel from place to place. Right now, about half a million people are up in the air somewhere.

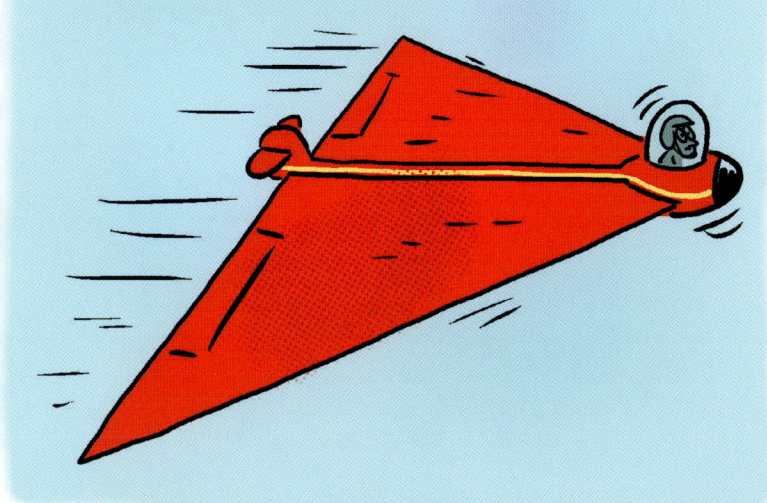

What went wrong?

The plane is pulled down to the ground by the force of gravity. Wings can make another force called lift which pushes the other way. For the plane to fly up off the ground, this lift force needs to be stronger than gravity.

Gravity is what stops us all floating up into air!

How does it work?

A wing has a special shape. The top is more curved than the surface underneath. When the wing slices through the air, the air flowing over the curved top has further to go to the get to the other side than the air travelling underneath. This difference makes the air on top of the wing move faster than the air below.

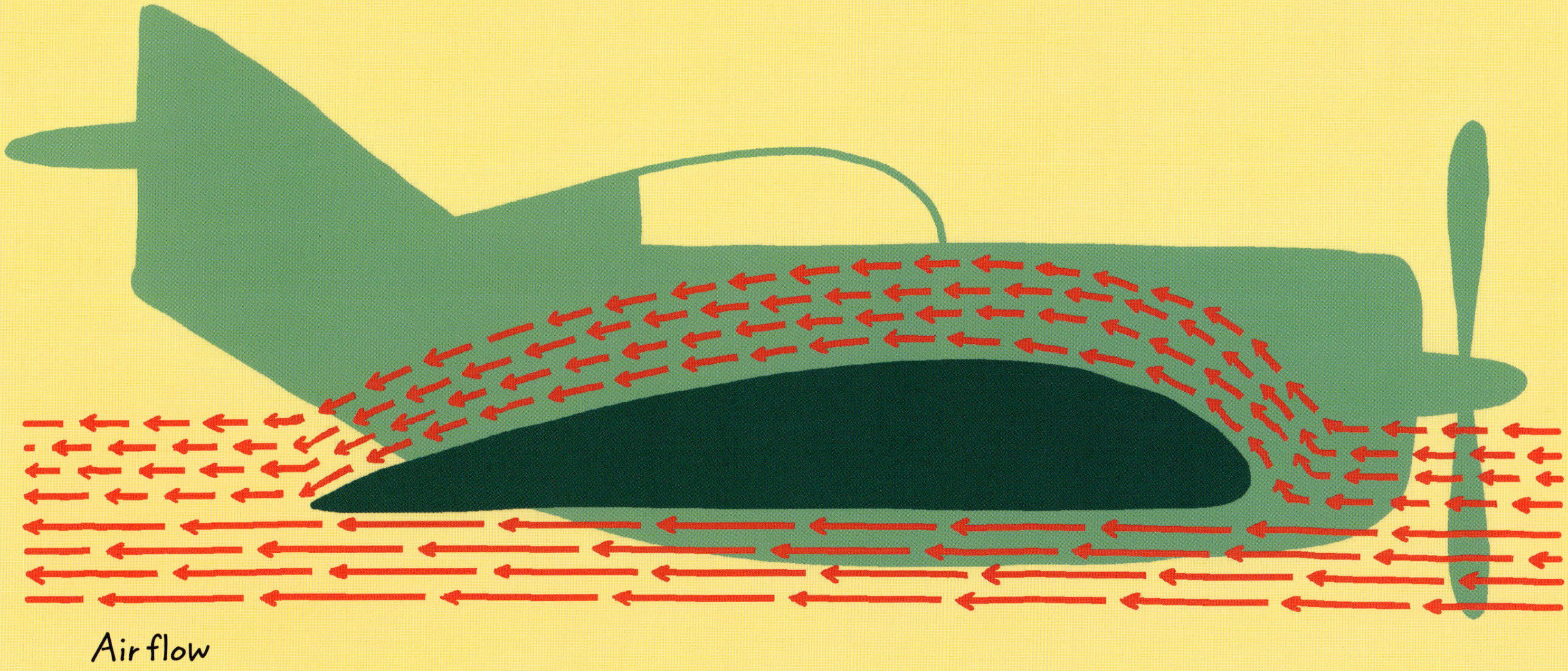

Air flow

Slow-moving air is less spread out than the faster air, and so it pushes up harder on the bottom of the wing than the air above pushes down. This difference makes the wing move up. And there we have it! We have lift!

What shall I make it with?

What went wrong?

The plane needs to be made of strong but lightweight material throughout. All planes have the same sections:

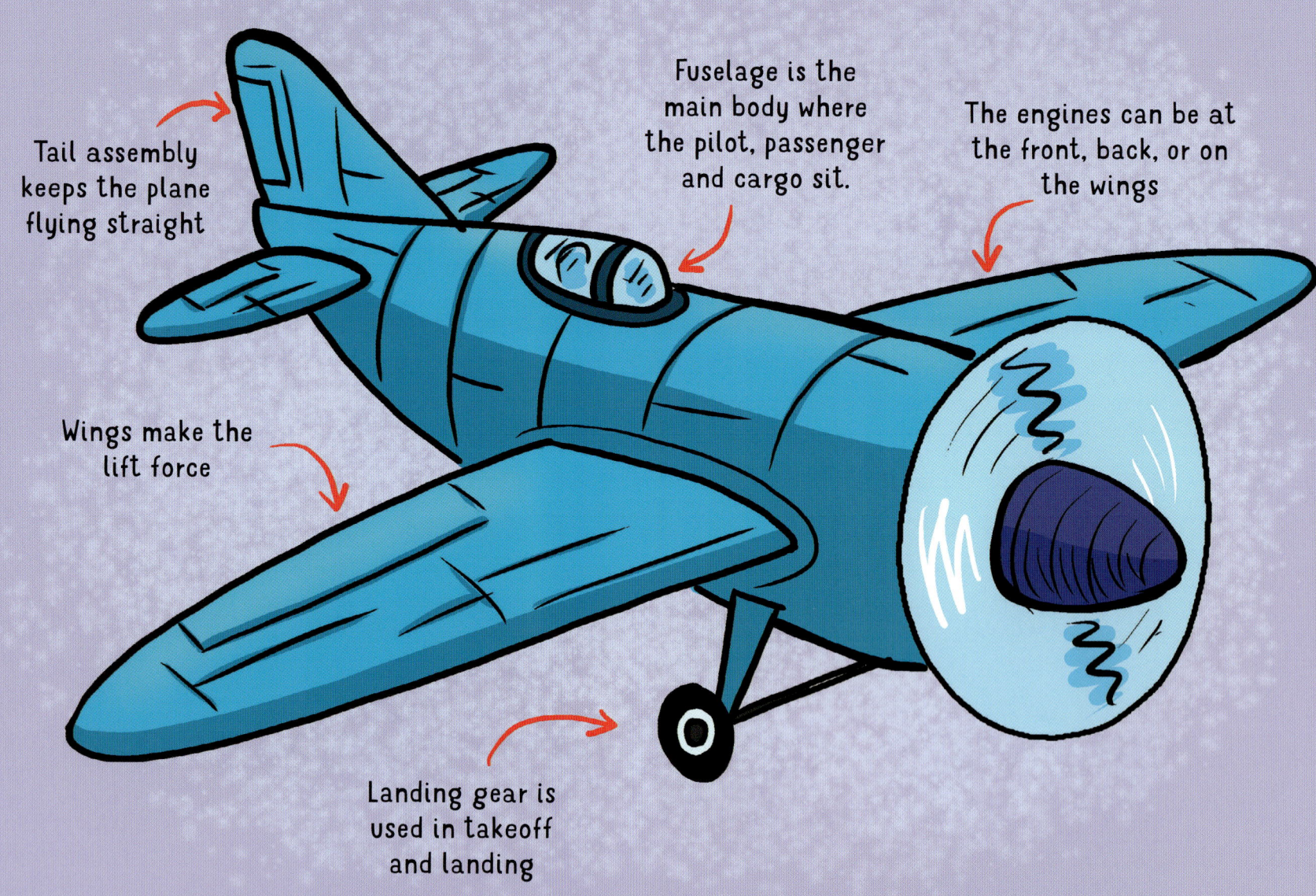

Tail assembly keeps the plane flying straight

Fuselage is the main body where the pilot, passenger and cargo sit.

The engines can be at the front, back, or on the wings

Wings make the lift force

Landing gear is used in takeoff and landing

How does it work?

A plane needs to be light in weight so its wings can lift it into the air easily. It also needs to be strong as it flies at very high speeds. The plane's body needs to be smooth and sleek so the air can flow around it without causing a lot of drag.

This means building an aircraft is complicated. The fuselage, wings and tail assembly have an internal frame. The frame is strong but not heavy.

For most jet planes, the frame is covered with curved aluminium panels. This metal is flexible and light. Small amounts of other metals, such as titanium, are mixed in to make the panels super strong.

The need for speed

What went wrong?

To fly, the plane wings needs a thrust force to push it through the air. The air pushes back with a force called drag. An engine is needed to provide a constant thrust so that the drag force does not slow the plane down to a stop. It won't fly at all if it stops!

A wing can only make lift when it is moving fast through air.

How does it work?

The fastest planes are powered with a jet engine. These suck in air at the front using a propeller-like fan. The fan also squeezes, or compresses, the air so it gets a bit hotter.

Further back in the engine, the warm air is mixed with a spray of fuel and that creates an explosion inside the combustion chamber. The explosion produces a blast of super-hot gas, which then whizzes out the back.

Just as the engine pushes the jet of hot gas out of the back, the jet of hot gas pushes back on the engine (and the rest of the plane), thrusting it forward.

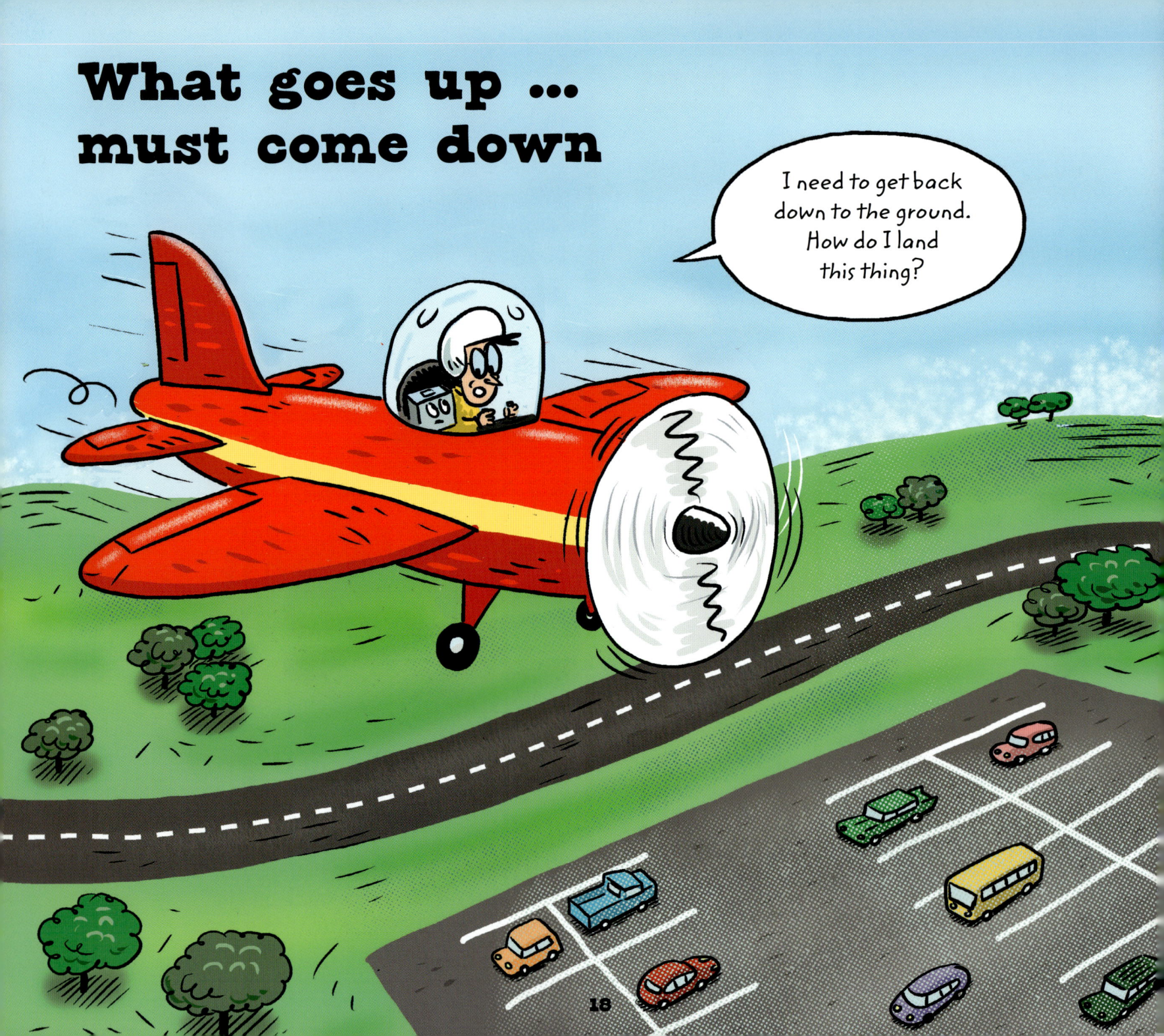

How does it work?

Wheels are the most common kind of landing gear. They are used by the fastest planes but only work safely on long smooth runways.

Seaplanes can land on water because they have large floats underneath. The water needs to be calm without too many waves.

A flying boat is not quite the same as a seaplane. It does not need landing gear because the whole thing floats!

Skiplanes can land on soft snow and slippery ice. The landing gear often has wheels that poke through the skis if needed so the pilot can land on normal runways too.

If it's good enough for a car...

Just paddle harder on one side?

This works with a boat.

This might take a lot of practice!

What went wrong?

Up in the air a plane can move in three separate ways.

Pitch: The nose of the plane tilts up or down. The pilot changes the pitch to make the plane climb or dive.

Yaw: The plane swivels around the middle as if it's on a merry-go-round. The wings stay flat.

Roll: The plane does not change direction but the wings tilt so the whole plane spins around even turning upside down. The pilot uses roll and yaw together to change the direction of the plane.

Urgh. It's making me feel sick just thinking about those moves!

How does it work?

The plane's wings and tail have moveable flaps called control surfaces. The pilot uses foot pedals and a control column to moves these flaps. They change the way air flows around the plane, and that makes the plane change position.

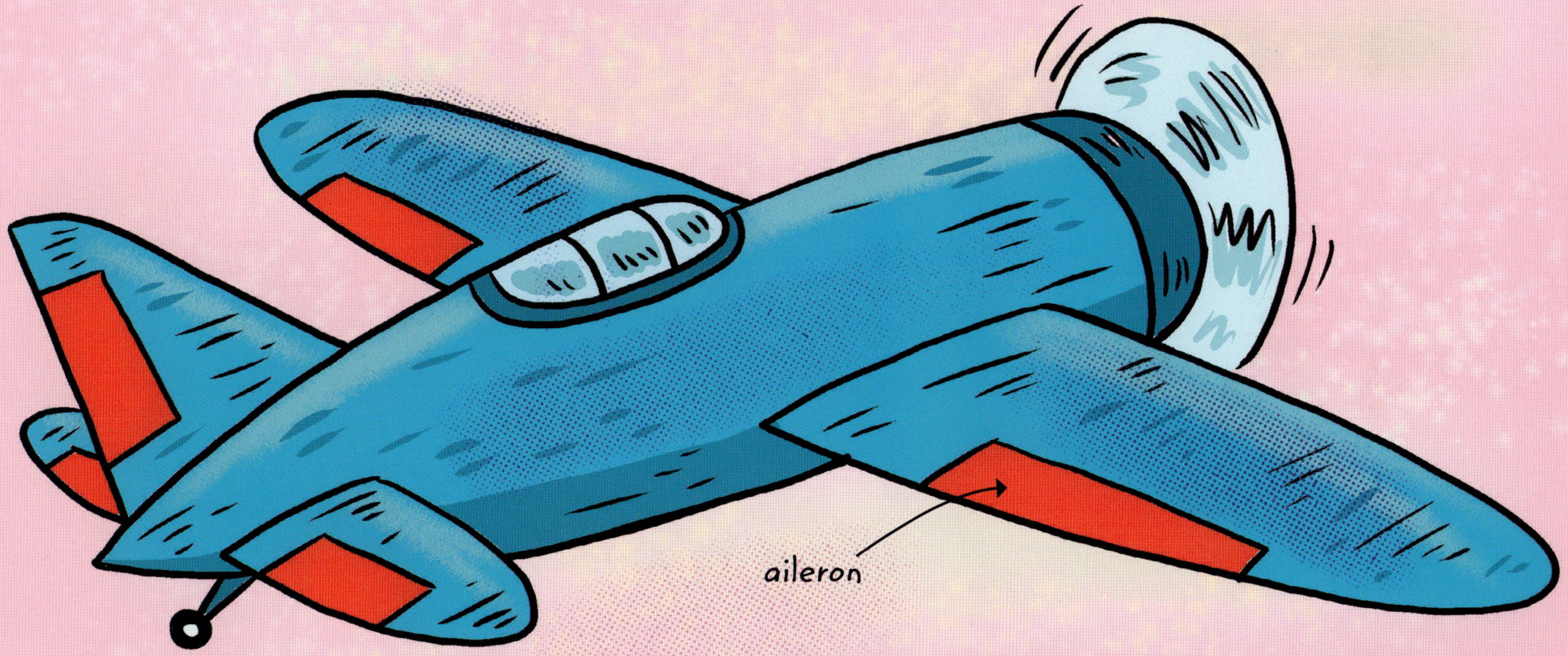

aileron

The ailerons control roll. Swing the control column to the left or right, but be gentle!

Wow, I can fly!

What makes a plane work?

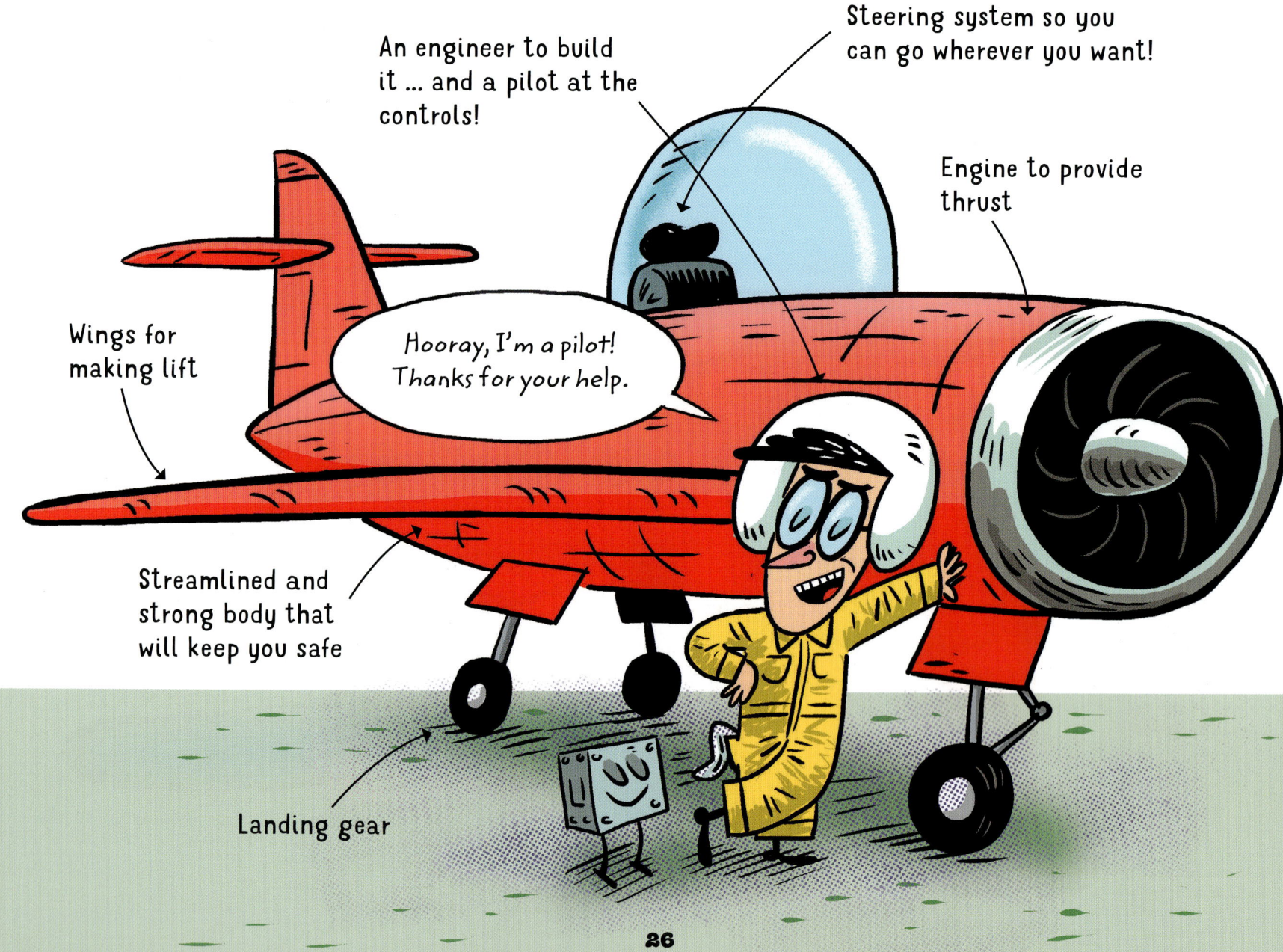

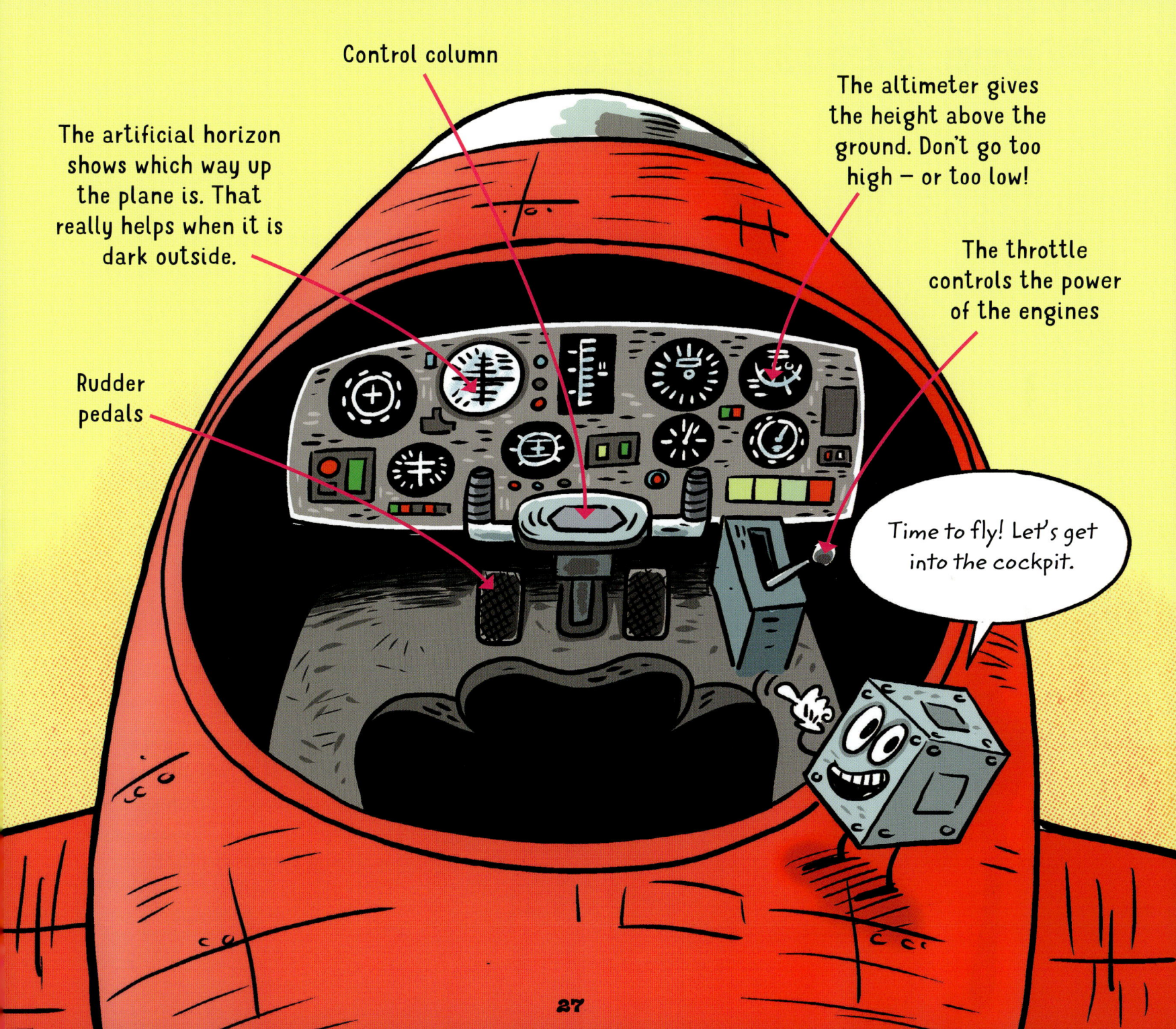

More flying machines

Hot air balloons: the hot air inside is very spread out so it floats upwards in colder air around it like a bubble in water.

Helicopters: the rotor blades are shaped like little wings. The spinning rotor makes a lift force that pulls the helicopter straight up.

Airship: The helium gas inside the airship is lighter than the air, so the whole aircraft floats in mid air.

How to become a pilot

- There is a minimum age in most countries before you can take flying lessons, normally 16 or 17 years old.
- Every learner must have many hours of lessons — about 25— and then fly solo (by themselves) for a total of 10 hours before they can qualify as a pilot.

- Airline pilots have to be older and have trained for much longer than this.

- Pilots must be checked by a doctor regularly to make sure they are healthy.

Quiz

So now you know how to build and fly a plane. Let's check your knowledge.

1. What is the force that pulls planes (and everything else) down to the ground.
A: Elastic bands
B: Gravity
C: A magnet

2. What is the main part of the plane called, where the pilot and passengers sit?
A: Fuselage
B: Tail
C: Engine

3. What cockpit controls are used to move the plane's rudder?
A: The red button
B: The throttle
C: The rudder pedals

Answers
1. B
2. A
3. C

Glossary

Drag - force that goes against a plane's motion in the air

Fuselage - the main body of a plane

Gravity - force (weight) of an object that draws things to the ground

Lift - force that opposes gravity and holds the plane in the air

Thrust - force created by a jet engine that moves an aircraft through the air

Index

ailerons 25
airship 28

engine 16-17

flying Boat 21

helicopter 28
hot air balloon 28

landing gear 21

materials 10-11

pilot 30
pitch 24

roll 24
rudder pedals 27, 29

sea plane 21
ski plane 21

thrust 16

wings 6-7, 9, 12, 13, 16, 25, 29

yaw 24